The Tyke Tiler Terrible Joke Book

Gene Kemp's first books, a series of stories about an amazing pig called Tamworth, immediately established her as one of the funniest and most imaginative authors writing for children. Then she wrote *The Turbulent Term of Tyke Tiler*, a ground-breaking school story which won the Library Association's Carnegie Medal and shot to the top of the children's bestseller lists. Others titles set in Cricklepit Combined School followed, along with collections of short stories, novels for teenagers, fiction for younger children and a powerful narrative poem, *The Mink War*. She is now recognized as one of the most popular contemporary children's authors, and she was awarded an honorary degree in 1984 in recognition of her achievement as a writer. She lives in Exeter, Devon.

THE TYKE TILER TERRIBLE JOKE BOOK

Gene Kemp

illustrated by Chris Fisher

ff

faber and faber

LONDON · BOSTON

First published in 1997
by Faber and Faber Limited
3 Queen Square London WC1N 3AU

Photoset by Avon Dataset Ltd, Bidford on Avon, Warwickshire
Printed in England by Mackays of Chatham plc, Chatham, Kent

A CIP record for this book
is available from the British Library

ISBN 0–571–17998–3

2 4 6 8 10 9 7 5 3 1

For Scroggins the Cat

Who died in November, a week after his
sixteenth birthday.
'A farewell miaow to the old hunter.'

and for Emily
the Joke-Bringer

CONTENTS

INTRODUCTION

Our school had a day off for staff meetings or something and I wandered over to look at my old school, Cricklepit Combined, to see how they were getting on with repairing the bell tower I'd wrecked. It was breaktime and kids were shouting and playing and running around as usual.

Suddenly a ball whizzed over the school fence and a chorus of voices sounded.

'Get us our ball back? Please!'

'OK,' I said, and kicked the ball. It flew over the fence and hit my old teacher Mr Merchant, who was on playground duty, on the back. He jumped round. Kids rushed away.

'Oh, crumbs,' I muttered, ready to run, but he'd seen me and began to walk towards the school gates where I was.

'Tyke,' he called. He was grinning now, so I stayed put. He'd always been OK.

'Sorry 'bout the ball, Sir,' I said. 'Accident. Honest.'

'It doesn't matter. How are you?' he asked. 'Come on in. I haven't seen you since you left Cricklepit.'

'I see they're doing up the school, Sir,' I said.

'Yes. It needed it. You probably did us a favour in the long run. Would you like to come in and visit the school as an old pupil? You're perfectly welcome. Come and see my class if you like.'

'Thanks, but no thanks, Sir. I wouldn't want to disturb your class.'

'All right, please yourself. Goodbye then.'

'Bye,' I said to his disappearing back, and stood for a moment lost in thought. Would I like to see his class? What a joke! Jokes. Now they were something I liked. I'd like to write about jokes. Jokes about schools and other things. So I took out a notebook and did a bit of scribbling.

'Oi,' said a voice. I looked round. A tough-looking kid scowled at me. 'You Tyke Tiler?'

'Yeah. What of it? And who are you?'

'Gowie Corby. I heard of you. You knocked down the tower, didn't you? Should've knocked down the whole school while you were at it.'

'I did me best!'

'What you writing about? Let me see.'

'Jokes. I'm gonna make a Joke Book.'

'I know lots of jokes. I'll help you.'

'I don't need any help, thank you.'

'Go on. I like jokes. Dirty and nasty ones.'

'I don't want dirty or nasty jokes, just funny ones.'

'Why not? Oh, all right. Look, I'll write some down and give you 'em.'

'OK. Here's where I live.' I wrote it down. 'I don't want to keep coming here too much.'

'See ya around.' He slouched away, still scowling.

I watched him but I then saw a familiar face, Ratbag Somers, my ancient enemy, walking across the playground in my direction so I walked out the gate and disappeared.

How else would you start a Joke Book but with school jokes?

I was caught writing some down in a French lesson and the teacher told me to stay in at lunchtime and write an essay about 'Not Writing Jokes in Class'. I thought for one horrible moment that I'd have to do it in French. But luckily English was OK. As I was doing it I wrote some more jokes.

Teacher: Can anyone give me a sentence with the word analyse in it?
Pupil: *Anna said she met the Spice Girls at a concert but Anna lies.*

Teacher: Jamie, tell me a sentence with the word fascinate in it.
Jamie: *My Dad has nine buttons on his waistcoat, but he can only fasten eight.*

Teacher: Now, Jane, if you had five pounds in your purse and you gave me one of them, what would you have?
Jane: *Someone else's purse, Sir.*

Teacher: Michael, if the supermarket was selling 20 bread rolls for £1 and I gave you 50 pence, what would you get?
Michael: *A very large bag of sweets.*

Teacher: Your homework is very good, Alan.
   Did your father help you?
Alan: No, Sir, he did it all.

Teacher: If you had £1 and you asked your
   Dad for another £1, what would you have?
Paul: Er . . . still £1, Sir.

Teacher: What would you do if a man-eating tiger was chasing you?
Joan: Nothing, 'cos I'm a girl.

Parent: Is my son really trying?
Teacher: Very!

Head: This is the fifth time you have been to see me this week. What do you have to say for yourself?
Boy: I'm certainly glad today's Friday.

Teacher: Why were you late for school?
Girl: There are eight people in our family and the alarm was set for seven.

Boy: I don't think I deserve a zero for my maths test.
Teacher: Neither do I, but it's the lowest mark I can give you.

Teacher: You missed school yesterday, didn't you?
Boy: Not at all.

Teacher: Dave, I hope I didn't see you looking at John's paper.
Dave: *I hope you didn't too.*

Why did the boy take a car to school?
To drive the teacher up the wall.

Why did the teacher wear sunglasses?
Because the class was bright.

Why should you take a hammer to school on
the last day of term?
It's breaking-up day.

What's the best place for the school sick-bay?
Next to the canteen.

Are you taking the school bus home?
No, my Mum would make me take it back.

Teacher: If Shakespeare were alive today, he'd
be a remarkable man.
Boy: *He certainly would. He'd be more than 300
years old.*

Teacher: Before we begin this exam, are there
any questions?
Girl: *What course are we doing?*

Teacher: You should have been here at nine.
Boy: Why? What happened?

What's the most popular sentence at school?
  I don't know!

SICK JOKES

I was at the doctors' for a check-up and since I got on well with him I told him some doctor jokes. He's all right, he is. But just before he finished his examination of me his face went quite serious.

'Tyke,' he said. 'I'm afraid I'm going to have to take some X-rays.'

I stopped laughing. 'Why? Is something wrong?'

'I'm afraid I might have to operate on you. Can you come this way?'

'Oh, no,' I whispered as I looked at his serious face.

It wasn't until I got to the door that he started grinning at me.

Doctor, Doctor, I feel like a packet of biscuits.
   What, square ones with holes in?
Yes, that's it.
   You must be crackers.

Doctor, Doctor, I think I'm blind.
   So do I. This is a fish-and-chip shop.

Doctor, Doctor, I feel like a parachute.
   Don't let it get you down.

Doctor, Doctor, I feel like a pair of curtains.
  Well, pull yourself together.

Doctor, Doctor, I feel like an apple.
  Come closer, I won't bite.

Doctor, Doctor, I feel like a pack of cards.
I'll deal with you in a minute.

Why do surgeons wear masks?
*So if they make a mistake no one will know
who did it.*

Doctor: I don't like the look of your husband.
Patient's wife: *I don't either but he is good to the
kids.*

Patient: Doctor, when I get well, will I be able
to play the piano?
Doctor: *I can't see why not.*
Patient: That's good. I've never played it before.

Doctor: I've got some good and bad news.
Patient: *What's the bad news?*
Doctor: We had to cut your feet off.
Patient: *And the good news?*
Doctor: The man in the next bed wants your
slippers.

Doctor: How is the child who swallowed the
£1 coin?
Nurse: *No change yet, Doctor.*

Doctor: I'm sure your wife misses you.
Bandaged patient: *No, she doesn't. That's why I'm here.*

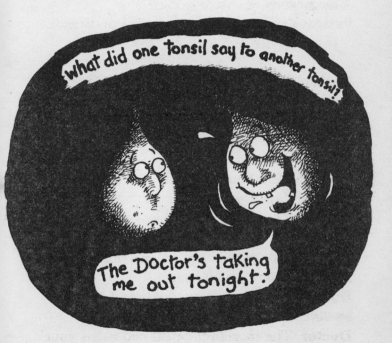

Patient: Help me, Doctor, I can't remember anything for more than a few minutes.
Doctor: *How long has this been going on?*
Patient: How long has what been going on?

Patient's wife: My husband has swallowed a fountain pen.

Doctor: I'll be right over. What are you doing in the meantime?

Patient's wife: In the meantime I'm using a pencil.

Doctor: You'll be all right. Your leg is a bit swollen but I wouldn't worry about it.

Patient: No, and if your leg was swollen I wouldn't worry about it either.

Receptionist: You'll find the Doctor very funny. I'm sure he'll have you in stitches.

Patient: I hope not. I only came for a check-up.

Doctor: I think your kleptomania should be cured by now, madam.

Patient: Thank you. Anything I could do for you?

Doctor: Well, if you should have a relapse I could do with a new car, thanks.

Doctor: You shouldn't drink on the job. I could tell the vicar.

Gravedigger: *Doc, I think you should be the last person to complain considering all the covering up I've done for you.*

ENERGETIC JOKES

'**F**it again, Tyke? Ready for the rugger team?' asked Mr Lively, our Games teacher.

'Don't know, Sir. I've not been meself recently.'

'Well, we'll soon find out. Five times round the running track for you. Off you go.'

I thought of plenty of jokes as I ran around plus loads of nasty thoughts about Games teachers.

Boy's mum: My son has got into the school football team.
Friend: What position does he play?
Boy's mum: Left back in the changing room.

Why wasn't Cinderella picked for the football team?
She kept running away from the ball.

Who carries the broom in a football team?
The sweeper.

Boy: I could kick myself for missing that penalty.
Team mate: Let me do it. You'll only miss again.

How do you keep cool at a football match?
Stand behind a fan.

Why is it a bad idea to go out with a tennis player?
Because love means nothing to them.

What happened to the karate expert who joined the Army?
He saluted and nearly killed himself.

Why do golfers wear two pairs of trousers?
>*In case they get a hole in one.*

What do boxers think the best part of a joke is?
>*The punchline.*

Why were the members of the cricket team given lights?
>*Because they kept losing all their matches.*

Why are you tired on April 1st?
>*You've just had a thirty-one day March.*

Drinker: Do you know how to make a fresh peach punch?
Barman: *Give her boxing lessons.*

Girl: You'd be a fine dancer except for two things.
Boy: *What are they?*
Girl: Your feet.

Boy in a boat: Dad, what are those holes in the bottom?

Dad: *Those are knotholes.*

Son: Well, if they're not holes, what are they?

What game do judges play?
> *Tennis – it's played in courts.*

THWACK!

Boy: I can swim with my head above the water.
Friend: So what? Wood floats.

Son: You've been working in the garden for hours. What are you growing?
Dad: Tired.

A fed-up football fan nailed his season ticket to the wall. Someone pinched the nail.

A football team's trophy room was raided and the entire contents were stolen. Police are currently looking for the club carpet.

Two canoeists were rowing down the Nile when suddenly a crocodile swam up and bit one of their feet off.
'Oh, no,' groaned the unlucky man. 'A crocodile's gone and bitten off my foot.'
'Which one?' asked the friend.
'I don't know – you've seen one crocodile and you've seen them all.'

'I was a nine-stone weakling,' a man said to his friend. 'When I went to the beach I got sand kicked in my face by bullies. So I took the Charles Atlas body-building course and now I weigh fourteen stone of solid muscle.'

'That's good,' said his friend.

'Not really,' the man went on. 'The last time I went to the beach a twenty-stone bully kicked sand in my face.'

One evening there came a ring on the doorbell. Mum answered it.

'Hello. Someone for you, Tyke,' she called. I went to the door and there stood Gowie Corby. Blimey, I'd forgotten about him.

'Come in,' I said. Gowie walked through the door and tripped head over heels over Crumble, who was getting in the way as usual. I pushed her away but she looked at Gowie and growled. Not love at first sight.

'You got any jokes then?' I asked, as we went into the kitchen. I shut the door to keep Crumble out.

'Yeah.' He produced a dirty, crumpled piece of paper. 'Some great ones here.'

Gowie couldn't keep his eyes off Spud's model of the Incredible Hulk.

'I like that.' he said, and squeezed the arm which promptly fell off.

I groaned. Spud was very proud of his model, which he'd just finished. I tried to fix it back on but it fell off again. At that moment the door opened and Spud came in, followed by Crumble who made a beeline or should I say dogline, for Gowie's trousers.

Then Spud noticed his Hulk model.

'Tyke,' he bawled. 'What have you done? It took ages making this!'

'It was me,' said Gowie, battling with Crumble. He shoved her away with his foot.

'Was it? Who are you coming in here wrecking my model and kicking the dog?' He and Gowie squared up to each other.

'It was an accident,' I said, trying to stand between them. Spud's bigger than Gowie.

'What's all this racket?' growled Dad, coming in. 'Spud, behave yourself!' Spud retreated, muttering.

'Gowie, I'm sorry,' I said. But Gowie had gone, walked out, vamoosed, vanished. I chased after him.

'I come round and your dog and your brother attack me,' he said after I'd caught him up. 'Nice family you've got.'

'Sorry. Thanks for the jokes anyway. Come round again if you've got some more.'

'You'll be lucky.'

'OK. I'll come round your place then.'

He thought about this, and for some reason a Tom-and-Jerry smile crossed his face. I hadn't seen him grin before.

'All right. Here's where I live. Come round next week sometime.'

Later I looked at his jokes, threw out half of them and put in some of my own.

What happened to the man who stole a
  calendar?
  He got twelve months.

Why did the policeman go up the tree?
  Because he was a special branch man.

Why did the convict steal a box of soap?
> *He wanted to make a clean escape.*

Why are policemen and policewomen strong?
> *Because they can hold up traffic.*

Did you hear about the fight in the fish-and-chip shop last night?
> *Two men got battered.*

Policeman: I'm going to lock you up tonight.
Man: What's the charge?
Policeman: There's no charge, it's all part of the service.

Man: The police are looking for a man with one eye called Mad Killer Jack.
Friend: What's his other eye called?

Robber: This is a hold-up. Give me your money or else.
Man: Or else what?
Robber: Don't confuse me, this is my first job.

Policeman: Did you steal this lady's rug?
Robber: No, she gave it to me and told me to beat it.

Boy: Officer, come quickly, my father's been fighting for half an hour.
Policeman: Why didn't you tell me before?
Boy: Because he was winning until a minute ago.

Why did the prisoner ask for a nice warm overcoat?
Because he had to spend the night in the cooler.

A man dialled 999. 'What service would you like: police or ambulance?' came the reply. 'Both,' said the man. 'I can't get my dog to open his mouth and there's a burglar inside.'

A bank had been robbed and the police asked if all the exits had been guarded.

'Yes,' said the security guard, 'but he must have gone out of the entrance.'

Judge: Constable, do you recognize this woman?

Constable: Yes, Sir. She approached me while I was in plain clothes and tried to pass this £20 note off on me.

Judge: Counterfeit?

Constable: Yes, Sir. She had two.

Policeman: Why are you trying to cross the road here? There's a zebra crossing just round the corner.

Pedestrian: Well, I hope the poor creature has better luck than I do.

'Is that the police?' asked a desperate voice.

'Yes, this is the police station,' came the reply.

'Oh, good. I want to report a burglar trapped in an old lady's house.'

'Who's this speaking?' asked the policeman.

'The burglar.'

There's a park in New York that's so dangerous
the muggers are demanding police
protection.

NUISANCE JOKES

These jokes are by my friend Danny, who had cottoned on to the fact that I was making a Joke Book.

'I know some good ones, Tyke. Really I do,' he pleaded in his special way.

He went on about it until I said yes. I didn't expect them to be very good, and they weren't.

'What do you think?' he said, his face shining with pride.

'They're great, Danny,' I said. His jokes weren't my cup of tea but some people like them, I suppose. Anyway, here they are.

What do you call a man with a seagull on his head?
   Cliff.

What do you call a man with a spade on his
   head?
   Doug.

What do you call a man without a spade on his
   head?
   Dougless.

What do you call a man with a car on his head?
   Jack.

What do you call a man with a lance in his
   head?
   Lance.

What do you call a man with ten lances in his
   head?
   Lancelot.

Knock, Knock.
   Who's there?
Knock, Knock.
   Who's there?
I'm sorry but my mother doesn't let me talk to
   strangers.

What do you call Batman and Robin if they
   had been run over by a steamroller?
     Flatman and Ribbon.

How many ears does Captain Kirk have?
     *Three – his left ear, his right ear and his final
     frontier.*

Where is Ben Nevis?
     Never heard of him.

Knock, knock.
> *Who's there?*

Ketchup.
> *Ketchup who?*

Ketchup with me and I'll tell you.

Knock, knock.
> *Who's there?*

Pecan.
> *Pecan who?*

Pecan someone your own size.

Knock, knock.
> *Who's there?*

Nicholas.
> *Nicholas who?*

Nicholas girls shouldn't climb trees.

Knock, knock.
> *Who's there?*

You're a lady.
> *You're a lady who?*

I didn't know you could yodel.

Knock, knock.
Who's there?
Adolf.
Adolf who?
A dolf ball hit me in de mouff and dats why I
dalk funny.

Knock, knock.
> *Who's there?*

Irish stew.
> *Irish stew who?*

Irish stew in the name of the law.

Knock, knock.
> *Who's there?*

Ivor.
> *Ivor who?*

Ivor got a letter for you.

Knock, knock.
> *Who's there?*

Woody.
> *Woody who?*

Woody come out if 'e knew who was
knocking?

Knock, knock.
> *Who's there?*

Amos.
> *Amos who?*

A mosquito just bit me.

Knock, knock.
> *Who's there?*

Lettuce.
> *Lettuce who?*

Lettuce in and you'll find out.

Knock, knock.
> *Who's there?*

Cook.
> *Cook who?*

That's the first I've heard this year.

Knock, knock.
> *Who's there?*

Soup.
> *Soup who?*

Souperman.

Knock, Knock.

I called these jokes awful 'cos quite simply I had an awful day. It was waste-collection day and my mother said she thought my jokes were just waste paper and had thrown them away.

So when I was supposed to be having breakfast and going to school, I was searching frantically through the rubbish. My jokes were at the bottom of a binliner, covered in old dog food, naturally.

Then I was late for school. That got me in trouble. And I had forgotten my P.E. kit. That got me in trouble. And I'd left my homework at

home. Which – surprise, surprise – got me in
trouble. 'Nuff said.

No wonder the general's angry. Someone sent
him a letter marked 'Private'.

Traveller: How much is a taxi to the station?
*Taxi driver: £2. The luggage goes for
nothing.*
Traveller: Right, take my luggage, I'll walk.

I've got a joke about dustbins, but it's rubbish.

What do misers do when it's cold?
Sit around a candle.
What do misers do when it's really cold?
Light the candle.

Heard about the man who bought a paper shop?

Yes, it blew away.

Why didn't the millionaire have any bathrooms in his mansion?

Because he was filthy rich.

Why did the lady drive her car off the cliff?

To test her air brakes.

Dave: I thought you were going to come round and fix the doorbell yesterday.

John: I did – I rang twice but you didn't answer.

Why are Saturday and Sunday the strongest days?

Because the others are weak days.

Boy: Does your watch tell the time?

Friend: No, you have to look at it.

Boy: Vicar, come quickly. The church is on fire.

Vicar: Holy smoke!

Which members of an orchestra can't you trust?
The fiddlers.

Why did the opticians go to the theatre?
Because it was a spectacle.

What can travel at the speed of sound yet has no legs, wings or engines?
Your voice.

Why is it useless to send a telegram to
  Washington?
  Because he's dead.

What kind of coat has no buttons and is always
  put on wet?
  A coat of paint.

What part of a car kills the most people?
  The nut behind the wheel.

Why is the farmer famous?
  Because he's outstanding in his field.

Why do you forget a tooth when it's been
  pulled?
  Because it goes right out of your head.

Why does lightning shock people?
  Because it doesn't know how to conduct itself.

What breaks but doesn't fall and what falls but
  doesn't break?
  *Dawn breaks but doesn't fall and night falls
  but doesn't break.*

What is the difference between a chicken and a person?

A person can get chickenpox but a chicken can't get personpox.

What did the oil painting say to the wall?

First they framed me, then they hung me.

How do you make a Venetian blind?

Poke him in the eye.

INDIGESTIBLE JOKES

One day I went into lunch late and didn't fancy what was left.

'No, thanks,' I said when it was offered. 'I'll just have pudding.'

The dinner lady took no notice and heaped it on to my tray. No bother, I'll just eat the pudding – which I did, but when I tried to put the rest in the big metal leftovers' bucket she stopped me.

'You must eat more than that,' she said.

I glared at her and sat down again. No way, I wouldn't serve that to Crumble and she eats nearly anything. I waited till no one was looking and tipped it on to the empty seat beside me and left with my empty tray. I didn't stay to find out whether anyone sat in it or not.

Waiter, there's a fly in my soup.
> *Don't worry sir, I won't charge you extra.*

Waiter, I'm in a hurry. Will the doughnuts be long?
> *No, sir. Round.*

Waiter, I found this button in the salad.
> *Sorry, sir. It must have come off while the salad was being dressed.*

Waiter, can I have a plate of soggy chips, undercooked eggs and burnt bacon?
> *I'm sorry, sir, we couldn't possibly give you anything like that.*

Why not? That's what I had yesterday.

'We always say prayers before we eat. Mum's a terrible cook.'

'You just don't appreciate good food.'
'I would if you ever cooked any.'

What's round, white and wears sunglasses?
A cool mint.

What's white, round and lifts very heavy
  weights?
  An extra strong mint.

'What are we eating?'
  'Let's eat up the street.'
'Oh, no, I hate concrete.'

'Have you ever seen a man-eating shark?'
  'No, but I've seen a man eating cod.'

A man fell into a vat of beer and came to a
  bitter end.

'What hand do you stir your coffee with?'
  'My right hand. Why?'
'I use a spoon.'

Why did the bakers go on strike?
  Because they wanted more dough.

How do you make an apple crumble?
  Hit it with a hammer.

'Son, why don't you wash your face? I can see
    what you had for breakfast today.'
'What was it?'
'Toast and jam.'
'Wrong, Dad, that was yesterday.'

Have you heard the joke about the butter?
    No. Tell it to me.
Better not, you might spread it.

Why do bananas use suntan oil?
    Because they peel easily.

Do you know the story about the Cornflakes?
No. Tell me about it.
I can't because it's a serial.

What's the definition of beetroot?
A potato with high blood pressure.

A man went to the butchers and was shocked
to see human arms and legs hanging from
hooks. 'That's horrible!' he exclaimed. 'Well,
what do you expect in a family butcher's
shop?' came the reply.

What's yellow and stupid?
Thick custard.

What kind of a motorbike can cook eggs?
A scrambler.

It was my turn to visit Gowie Corby that evening. I didn't really want to, but I'd promised. He lived quite near in a cul-de-sac with some run-down houses. I found his number and rang the bell twice. No sound or reply. I checked again. Was he out? Then I saw the notice on the door.

'Bell doesn't work. Let yourself in.' I entered warily and called his name. A kind of muffled reply. I called again. The same noise. I walked through the silent house with goose bumps on my skin.

'Gowie, Gowie,' I called, and it echoed through the house. Then I saw a light at the bottom of the stairs. He must be down there.

'Gowie.' Louder this time. I entered a room which was like a cellar. No, he wasn't there. Suddenly the door slammed and the light went out. I shouted loudly. No reply this time. I tried the door handle. It didn't turn.

Then I heard this scratching sound and saw some mice running around. Normally mice don't bother me but in this dark place they did. Figures stood all around me. Horror figures – Dracula, Frankenstein, werewolves, mummies.

'Help!' I yelled. Was Gowie playing tricks? I couldn't be certain. Was I in the right house? Terror zoomed through my brain. And then a horrible screeching started, like someone scraping their fingernails down a blackboard. A nightmare, I thought. I'm in a nightmare. Why did I come here? I didn't have to. Everyone says Gowie's trouble, danger. I was scared sick.

And then the light came on, and a girl's voice said, 'All right, Count Dracula, that's enough. A joke's a joke.'

The door opened and Gowie stood there grinning wickedly, holding a violin. Beside him stood a tall black girl. I knew her. She was Rosie Lee, Gowie's friend. His only friend.

'Hello, Tyke. Didn't scare you, did I?' grinned Gowie.

'Yes, you did, you rotten pig.'

'Quits now. I had a lousy time at your house so we're evens now. No hard feelings.'

Rosie Lee grinned at me. She seemed quite normal but then she did call him Count Dracula for some reason. A friend of Gowie's would be mad anyway.

We went through to the kitchen and looked at his jokes. But it wasn't long before I split. The house was spooking me.

I had just left to get back home when I saw three large, menacing figures sitting on motorbikes outside the house.

That was the last straw. I took to my heels and fled down the road, away from Gowie's house from hell.

Tourist: You say you have a ghost that walks at midnight?
Guide: Yes, the last bus goes at 11.30.

Why do witches like English lessons?
Because they're good at spelling.

Do monsters eat popcorn with their fingers?
No, they eat the fingers separately.

Why didn't the ghost go to the dance?
She had no body to go with.

What did the monster eat after the dentist took all his teeth out?
The dentist.

What is a cannibal's favourite meal?
Kate and Sidney pie.

What dances do vampires like?
The Fangdango.

Why did they put a fence around the graveyard?
Because people are dying to get in.

Two vampires met on a dark night in Transylvania. One of them said, 'Like a game of vampires?'
'What do you want to play that for?' asked the other.
'Oh, for very high stakes.'

Why did the witches go on strike?
Because they wanted electric brooms.

A vicar was speaking to a condemned man on the electric chair.
'Is there any last thing I can do for you?' he asked.
'Yes,' said the prisoner. 'Hold my hand.'

Missionary: Why are you looking at me that way?
Cannibal: I am a food inspector.

Why do witches fly through the air on
   broomsticks?
   Because vacuum cleaners are too heavy.

First cannibal: Am I late for dinner?
Second cannibal: Yes, everyone's eaten.

Mother cannibal to boy cannibal: How often have I told you not to speak with someone in your mouth.

Mother cannibal to father cannibal: I'm worried about Junior. He wants to be a vegetarian.

Missionary to clever cannibal: Do you mean to say you've been to university yet you still eat people?
Cannibal: Yes, but now I use a knife and fork.

A man was exploring the jungle when he was spotted by a tribe of cannibals who caught him and brought him back to their camp for the Chief's dinner. As he was being placed in the cauldron the Chief asked him, 'What job do you do?'
'I'm Assistant Editor on a newspaper,' said the unlucky man, sadly.
'Oh, well, cheer up,' said the Chief. 'Soon you'll be Editor in Chief.'

Cannibal: I've got really bad stomach-ache today.

Witch doctor: What have you eaten?

Cannibal: Bald man, dressed in brown and wearing sandals.

Witch doctor: How did you cook him?

Cannibal: I boiled him.

Witch doctor: No wonder you've got stomach-ache, he was a friar.

What can you say about someone who escapes from cannibals only to meet a lion?

Out of the frying pan and into the fire.

One evening I took Crumble for a walk in the fields. I told her some doggy jokes which she seemed to understand and she woofed at me from time to time. She was fine until we passed this man walking along with a male mongrel dog which looked like a cross between a labrador and a sheepdog.

It was love at first sight, with much sniffing and rubbing going on. I had to pull Crumble away and the man did likewise with his dog. Crumble gave a lovesick howl as they walked away.

I waited until they disappeared before I let go of Crumble's collar. That was a mistake. Like a streak of lightning she was off, heading in their direction.

'Crumble,' I bellowed after her. By the time I'd reached the spot where I'd last seen her nobody was there. I hunted high and low but there was no sign of her. Sick as a parrot I walked home, wondering what to say to Mum and Dad. They'd say I should have kept her on the lead.

But just as I turned into our street a happy, wagging figure joined me.

'You bad dog. Don't you ever do that again,' I scolded her.

She jumped up at me and barked happily as if it were all a joke.

How do you get four elephants in a Mini?
   Two in the front, two in the back.
How do you get four hippos in a Mini?
   You can't, it's full of elephants.

What kind of dog keeps the best time?
   A watchdog.

What kind of dog has got no tail?
  A hot dog.

If a dog loses his tail where does he get another one?

At a re-tail shop.

Why do birds fly south?

Because it's too far to walk.

What's worse than raining cats and dogs?

Hailing taxis.

What do you get if you cross a kangaroo with an elephant?

Big holes in Australia.

What do you get if you sit underneath a cow?

A pat on the head.

What do you call a blind deer?

No eye deer.

Why did the bald man put rabbits on his head?

Because at a distance they would look like hares.

Why did the cat want to join the Red Cross?

It wanted to be a First Aid Kit.

What happened when the cat swallowed the penny?
There was money in the kitty.

Why didn't the piglets listen to their father?
Because he was such a boar.

What did the circus say to the naughty elephant?
Pack your trunk and get out.

What has more lives than a cat?
A frog – it croaks every night.

How do you hunt bear?
Take all your clothes off.

What do you get if you pour hot water down a
   rabbit hole?
   Hot cross bunnies.

What do you get if you cross a kangaroo with a
   sheep?
   A woolly jumper.

When is it unlucky to cross the path of a black cat?
When you're a mouse.

How do you stop a mole digging up your garden?
Hide the spade.

What do you call a camel at the North Pole?
Lost.

How do you write a letter to a fish?
You drop him a line.

I was trying to think of a title for my Joke
Book. I came up with *Tyke Tiler's Revolting
Riddles* or *Tyke Tiler's Painful Puns*. No, they
weren't quite right. I thought harder and finally
came up with *The Tyke Tyler Terrible Joke Book*.
Great. That would do fine.

Since I was going to call it that, I thought
that one of the sections ought to be called
'Terrible Jokes'. Besides which, the jokes *are*
pretty bad.

Why did the chicken cross the road?
To get to the other side.

Why did the elephant cross the road?
Because it was the chicken's day off.

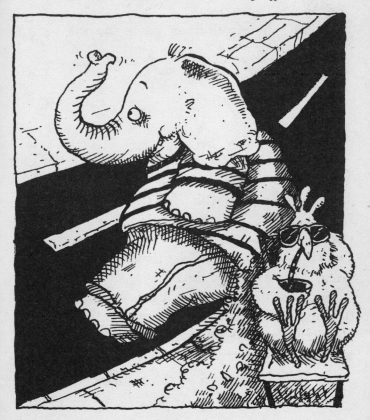

Why did the chicken cross the road again?
For fowl purposes.

Why did the chewing gum cross the road?
Because it was stuck to the chicken's feet.

What did the big chimney say to the little chimney?
You're too young to smoke.

Why did the dinosaur cross the road?
Because chickens weren't around then.

Why did the man with one hand cross the road?
To get to the second-hand shop.

What did the big telephone say to the little telephone?
You're too young to be engaged.

What did the traffic light say to the lamppost?
Don't look now, I'm changing.

How many feet are there in a yard?
It depends how many people are in it.

Why did the lady sit on her watch?
Because she wanted to be on time.

Why did the boy chuck the clock out of the window?
Because he wanted to see time fly.

Why did the boy scout get dizzy?
> *He did too many good turns.*

What long word has just one letter in it?
> *An envelope.*

What travels round the world yet stays in one corner?
> *A postage stamp.*

What do you get if you cross the sea with your mind?
> *Brain waves.*

What road has diamonds down the middle?
> *The jewel carriageway.*

What is big, has four wheels and flies?
> *A rubbish cart.*

How can you make trousers last?
> *Make the jacket first.*

What is the best room to go to if you are dying?
> *The living room.*

Have you heard about the man with two left
    ears?
    He couldn't hear right.

Did you hear about the man who always had
    aeroplanes outside his house?
    He used to leave the landing lights on.

Why do shoes go to heaven?
    Because they have soles.

Did I tell you the joke about the high wall?
    Better not, you'll never get over it.

Why did the girl take a pencil to bed?
> *To draw the curtains.*

What goes up but never comes down?
> *Your age.*

Why do dentists wear braces?
> *To keep their trousers up.*

Why did the farmer run a steamroller over his potato patch?
> *Because he wanted mashed potato.*

What goes in a field and makes music?
> *Pop corn.*

How do you make seven even?
> *You take the S away.*

Why is a river rich?
> *Because it has two banks.*

DREADFUL JOKES

I was supposed to be doing homework but I was doing my jokes in the front room instead. Dad came in, so I quickly put them inside the daily paper and picked up my maths book. To my horror, Dad picked up the paper and took it to the fireplace where he was about to start a fire. We had an open one in our house to cut down on the heating bills.

'You finished with this paper?' he asked me.

'No, no, I'm still reading it,' I said, and zoomed out of my chair to snatch the paper from him.

'Steady on. It's only a paper, not the crown jewels.'

Phew!, I thought, as he left the room to get another paper. That was a dreadful moment. That's what I'll call these jokes. Dreadful.

When a mother came home from work she was
    horrified to find her son throttling their pet
    rabbit. 'What are you doing?' she cried.
The son said, 'Well, my teacher told me that
    rabbits could multiply brilliant but this one
    can't even answer 2 times 2.'

Two friends who lived in a town were chatting.
    'I've just bought a pig,' said the first.
'But where on earth will you keep it?' asked the
    second.
'Your garden's much too small for a pig.'
'I'm going to keep it under my bed,' replied the
    first.
'But what about the smell?'
'The pig'll soon get used to that.'

What's a complete waste of time?
Telling a bald man a hair-raising story.

A boy was talking to his miserable friend in the
    playground. 'What's up?' he asked him.
'Well, two weeks ago my grandad gave me
    £20.'
'What's wrong with that?' asked the boy.
'And last week my uncle gave me £10.'
'Well, then, what are you so upset about?'
'Because this week so far I've got nothing.'

Customer: How much is a haircut?
Barber: Two pounds.
Customer: How much is a shave?
Barber: One pound.
Customer: Shave my head, please.

Two men met at the Job Centre. One said to
    the other, 'Did you get that job as a
    gravedigger?'
'No,' said the other man. 'I turned it down.'
'Why's that?'
'I thought it would be a bit of a dead end job.'

A famous comedian was once sent to entertain
the Prime Minister at No. 10 Downing
Street. 'I'll tell you all the latest jokes, sir,'
He said to the Prime Minister. 'No need,'
said the Prime Minister. 'I have already
appointed them in the Cabinet.'

Two football nuts, Dave and John, are climbing a telegraph pole outside the ground to try and get a better view of the match when John falls down and injures his leg. 'Support my leg,' says John, so Dave goes, 'John's leg, John's leg, John's leg!'

An underpaid worker went to see his boss about a rise.
'Why should I?' asked his boss.
'Well, I've got plenty of companies interested in me,' said the worker. 'The gas company, the water company, the electric company.'

Good jokes to end the book on. Finish on a happy note, peace and goodwill to all men, that sort of thing – though I know that doesn't apply to everyone. For instance, somehow I didn't think Gowie Corby would have a very happy Christmas. Still, for a lot of people it's a happy occasion. I usually quite enjoy my Christmas.

Spud hid my presents for a joke last year. I'm going to play a trick on him this time, if I can think of one.

'Hey, Mum, you know that incredible waterproof, shockproof, dustproof, burglar-proof, all-singing, all-dancing unbreakable watch you gave me for Christmas? Well, I lost it.'

Grandma gave me a present to help me stop biting my nails. It was a pair of shoes.

Last year I gave my baby brother measles for Christmas.

'What's two foot long, has a hundred hairy legs and goes GLOOP, GLOOP, GLOOP?'
  'I don't know.'
'I don't know either but that's what you're getting for Christmas.'

What do you give a railway stationmaster for Christmas?
Platform shoes, of course.

Auntie gave me a dictionary for Christmas. I was so pleased I couldn't find the words to thank her.

'Dad, Jim's broken my new doll.'
'How did he do that?'
'I hit him on the head with it.'

'I've just eaten the wishbone.'
'Are you choking?'
'No, I'm deadly serious.'

Why aren't elves allowed their Christmas lunch?
Because they're always goblin their food.

'Our cat doesn't eat turkey on Christmas day.'
'Why not? Cats love turkey.'
'I know, we just don't give it any.'

Dad said it would be best if Mum didn't eat much over Christmas. Mum said she'd rather have second best, thank you very much.

When Santa got to England he got stuck in a chimney. Now he's the toast of London.

One Christmas Eve a policeman found a man
on the pavement who'd been knocked over.
'Did you get the car's registration number?'
asked the policeman.
'No,' said the man, 'but I'd recognize those
reindeer anywhere.'

How many chimneys does Santa have to climb
down on Christmas Eve?
Stacks.

What did the reindeer say to Santa when he
told him a joke?
This one will sleigh you.

Tina always puts a great big arrow next to her
house so that Santa won't forget to visit.
'But he always comes,' said her Mum.
'I know,' said Tina. 'It works every time.'

Did you hear about the twins who were so
close that they hung up a pair of tights for
Santa?

Jim got a brand new bicycle for Christmas. As
   he whizzed down the hill he called out,
   'Look, Tina, no hands.' As the bike picked
   up speed he called out, 'Look, Tina, no feet.'
   As he crashed into the back of a lorry he
   called out, 'Look, Tina, no teef.'

Grandad was in a shop looking at train sets.
'Your grandson would love to have a set like
   that one,' said the salesman.
'You're dead right,' said Grandad. 'In that case
   I'd better have two sets.'

'I know you wanted that trumpet for
   Christmas, but if you don't stop playing it
   I'm going to go crazy.'
'But, Dad, I stopped playing it half an hour
   ago.'

I shot round to Cricklepit straight after school hoping to meet Gowie on neutral ground with my now complete Joke Book in a new folder. I didn't want to but he had a right to see it, I suppose.

Soon he appeared. I showed him the Joke Book and he thumbed through the pages.

I didn't bother to ask him what he thought when I saw his face. It was even blacker than usual.

'What a load of rubbish!' he said. 'Where are all the good jokes I gave you?'

'They were unprintable. I couldn't put them in a book,' I protested.

'Why not? Better than that stuff in there.' He chucked the Joke Book on the ground and kicked it away. Some of the pages spilled out.

Something snapped inside me and I hit him. So he clouted me back and then we started slugging it out in the playground, fists flying, boots swinging. He's bigger, but I'm older. Kids gathered round, cheering us on.

Then an unwelcome face showed itself, none other than Mrs Somers, my ancient enemy.

'Stop it at once!' she shouted. We parted and glared at each other. 'Gowie Corby, go to the Headmaster's office at once. And *you*,' she said to me, 'shouldn't be here! Get out of this school now or I'll call the police!'

Full of hate, I bent down to pick up my folder and its scattered pages. Gowie grabbed a few sheets and tore them as he walked off with a face like a thundercloud.

'Come back and pick them up first,' Mrs Somers shouted after him.

'Don't worry. I will,' I said, picking up my precious bits and pieces of paper.

It took me half the weekend to mend the

pages and put them back in order. But it was worth it, I thought, looking at my Joke Book. Well, I like it. I think it's great even if you don't. Cheers.